Original title:
Buttons on the Breeze

Author: Helena Marchant
ISBN HARDBACK: 978-1-80586-174-4
ISBN PAPERBACK: 978-1-80586-646-6

A Tapestry of Memory on the Wind

A kite once flew with sparkly thread,
It tangled with a cat named Red.
They danced around, both giggled in glee,
As squirrels watched, laughing from a tree.

A paper hat took flight one day,
It landed where the chickens play.
They strutted proud, wore it with flair,
Clucking jokes with a pinch of air.

A sock flew off, its partner shy,
It waved goodbye, then said, 'Oh my!'
A chicken chased it near the fence,
While neighbors laughed, it made no sense.

With every twist, the laughter swells,
A fluttering dance, oh how it tells!
Of silly things that took to flight,
Chasing joy from morning till night.

Dandelions and Story Threads

In the field, they dance and sway,
Fluffy seeds in bright array.
Whispers tell of tales of old,
As stories sprout from little gold.

Laughter carried with the wind,
Chasing dreams, they'll never end.
Somersaults through verdant glee,
Life's a yarn, come spin with me!

The Playful Waltz of Anything Small

Tiny things that laugh and twirl,
A pebble jumps, a roly-poly girl.
In a pocket, secrets hide,
Each one has its own wild ride.

Through the grass, they leap and cheer,
Whimsical tales that draw you near.
Catch a glimpse before they flee,
Oh, what fun it is to see!

Discoveries Carried on Gentle Currents

Drifting paper boats on streams,
Chasing hopes and wild dreams.
Floating toys from days of yore,
Tales of mischief on the shore.

Currents giggle as they play,
Nudging secrets on their way.
Each splash whispers with delight,
As laughter dances, taking flight!

Enigmas Woven by the Sky

Clouds stretch out, a jester's smile,
Knitting puzzles all awhile.
Rainbows peek from fluffy seams,
Casting shadows, chasing dreams.

Mysteries swirl in the blue,
Bubbles float, drifting anew.
Every wink of sun's warm light,
Teasing thoughts in playful flight!

Lullabies of Forgotten Fasteners

In the attic, treasures hide,
A mismatched lot, they laugh and sigh.
Tiny circles, memories shear,
Tales of stitches, forgotten cheer.

A plastic dude with a funky grin,
Winks at me, where do I begin?
Old fabric friends, they dance and sway,
In a lullaby, they drift away.

Nature's Choir of Colorful Tales

The garden's filled with hues so bright,
As daisies hum and lilies delight.
A patchwork quilt of giggles loud,
Nature’s laughter, wearing a shroud.

With every breeze a tiny cheer,
Fastened hearts feel nothing but clear.
Petals whisper, secrets unfold,
Tales of warmth in colors bold.

Airborne Dreams Adorned in Fabric

In the sky, a parade of cloth,
Flying high, they look so froth.
Each flutter sends a wink or two,
Tales of magic, stitched anew.

As kites join in their happy play,
With threads of laughter on display.
Floating dreams in the sunlight beam,
Adorned in whims, we all can dream.

Light as Air, Bright as Memory

A feather's fall, a giggle's call,
Resting softly, it floats and sprawls.
Mirrored laughter, sharp and clear,
Whimsical moments, oh so dear.

Chasing shadows, they spin and weave,
Tickled fancies that we believe.
Each tale a thread, bright and spry,
In our minds, forever they fly.

Enigmatic Marks in the Fabric of Air

Tiny round wonders flutter and sway,
Joking with clouds on a bright, sunny day.
They giggle and twist in a delicate race,
Drawing smiles on the faces of those in their space.

Twisted and harried, they jump and they spin,
Chasing the whispers of laughter within.
What secrets they hold in their colorful flight,
Painted in twilight, all silly and bright.

Whimsy Nestled Among the Leaves

Amidst the green, there's a whimsical sight,
Round little characters, pure energy and light.
Hopping through branches, they jingle and jive,
Making the forest feel wildly alive.

They play silly games with the chill in the air,
Spinning and twirling without a single care.
The leaves join the fun, in a rustling thrill,
While the sun chuckles down with a warm-hearted spill.

The Dance of Untethered Keepsakes

Little treasures set free on a whimsical quest,
Floating and flailing, they giggle with zest.
Each fleeting moment a chance to collide,
With joy in their hearts as they swirl and they glide.

They swoosh past the rooftops, they twirl past the trees,
Unlocking the laughter, stirring up glee.
A kaleidoscope chaos, full of bright cheer,
Igniting the sky with a wink and a leer.

Chronicles of Airborne Memories

In the sky, old tales of laughter unite,
Bouncing and swirling from morning till night.
Their snickers echo, as they drift on the breeze,
Weaving through sunshine with effortless ease.

Legends of joy take their flight in a whirl,
Stories of mischief, each twirl's like a pearl.
A tapestry woven from giggles and cheer,
The echoes of fun forever endear.

The Art of Floating Adornments

Tiny orbs on the flutter,
Dance like they found a new nutter.
In the wind they swirl and sway,
Laughing as they float away.

Snagged on a tree's gentle bough,
They twirl like kids without a vow.
Chasing tails of a rolling kite,
A playful sight, pure delight.

Each color bright with glee and cheer,
Whispers secrets we can't hear.
What tales they carry from afar,
Adventures near, under the star!

A whimsical, splendid parade,
As joys of life are whisked and laid.
Fleeting moments, time will tease,
In the air, like whimsical pleas.

Whims of Forgotten Closets

Old treasures gather dust and grime,
Whispers of a long lost rhyme.
Hanging proudly, with flair and pride,
They giggle at the dreams inside.

Pants with patches, shirts so bright,
Socks unmatched, a silly sight.
Their stories spill with every nudge,
Reminding us to never judge.

In shadows deep, they plot and scheme,
To relive days of dance and dream.
Together, they toast with hidden cheer,
A fashion show of yesteryear.

Each corner holds a tale or two,
Of socks that vanished, of pants askew.
They're a comedy of clashing hues,
Forgotten gems, we once did choose.

Elysian Dreamscapes of Ties

Ties that twist and comically bend,
Stories hanging at each vibrant end.
Swirling colors in disarray,
They sway around in a jolly play.

A polka dot sings to a striped mate,
Arguing who'll choose the best date.
A bowtie winks with a smirk so sly,
As necks above roll their eyes to the sky.

In boardrooms dull, they lead a dance,
Fumbling folds in a merry prance.
Choking on laughs, the bosses partake,
While ties spin tales for humor's sake.

Each knot a riddle of fabric and flair,
Wrinkled dreams of a whimsical air.
When worn with pride, they laugh with ease,
A snapshot of what fashion believes.

The Ballad of Frayed Edges

Frayed hemlines play a silly tune,
Dancing beneath the blissful moon.
Each twist and turn, a story spins,
Of wardrobe woes and cherished sins.

Lop-sided seams have much to share,
They tug at threads with crafty flair.
Torn pockets filled with ancient gum,
Whispering woes, ‘Why are we dumb?’

They waddle down a fashion street,
Making sure to dodge the beat.
In the style world, they laugh and tease,
‘We hold the treasure, if you please!’

A patchwork life with tales to tell,
Of moments lived so very well.
Frayed edges laugh, defy the norm,
In their chaos, they find their form.

The Artistry of Fabric-Free Freedom

A shirt flew high, oh what a sight,
Dancing alone, in the broad daylight.
An old sock joined, in a whirlwind spin,
Sewed chaos laughed, 'Let the fun begin!'

With no one wearing, they rule the air,
Giggling garments with not a care.
A vest declared, 'I feel so free!'
To twirl with socks in a jubilee.

Celestial Clusters of Color

A rogue red tie caught a breeze,
Twirling past trees with elegant ease.
Yellow shorts spun, fueled by the sun,
With laughter and joy, oh what fun!

A polka-dot blouse joined the parade,
In a sunny dance, never afraid.
They soared as meteors, wild in the sky,
As passersby chuckled, wondering why.

The Harmony of Wind and Fabric

One windy day, a hat took flight,
Bobbing and weaving, what a delight!
Scarf and glove started a race,
They looped and swirled in a fabric chase.

Out of the closet, they ran to play,
The sun was shining, it's a perfect day.
Muffled giggles from unseen threads,
While socks whispered tales of yarns and spreads.

Curious Twirls of Gentle Lightness

A lone sock waved to a breeze so kind,
With mismatched dreams, a tale unlined.
A t-shirt shouted, 'Let's dance carefree!'
As sunlight draped them in jubilee.

Together they spun, twirling with glee,
As if they were kids, wild, bold, and free.
The playful air sang tunes of delight,
As cloth and laughter took dazzling flight.

Floating Remnants of a Daydream

In a field of fluffy whispers,
They float like silly thoughts,
Bouncing off the daisy heads,
And giggling in their spots.

A stray breeze, a playful flirt,
Twirling leaves in joyous jest,
As shadows chase the meadow's pranks,
Inviting whimsy to their quest.

The sky winks at the jesters,
With clouds that laugh and tease,
Each twist a fleeting echo,
Dancing lightly with the breeze.

The Gentle Pull of Nostalgic Ties

Socks forgotten on the line,
Waving like a pirate's flag,
Each gust a whisper of the past,
A childhood without lag.

In twilight's soft embrace we find,
Our memories take their flight,
Toward realms of forgotten giggles,
In the fading of the light.

Echoes of our foolish deeds,
Tethered to the joyous earth,
As laughter dances in the air,
Reminding us of our mirth.

Sundry Shapes in the Wind's Embrace

Kites that zigzag on a whim,
Chasing clouds in dizzy loops,
They dart and dive in playful style,
Becoming wayward, silly troops.

A hat caught in a playful gust,
Flips and flutters in delight,
As giggles weave through every flake,
Making ordinary life feel light.

Shapes appear and vanish fast,
Like secrets tucked in around,
Laughter spills as petals twirl,
In lively dance, the earth is crowned.

A Carousel of Extravagant Absences

The whims of absence spin around,
In a circus of the bizarre,
Each memory a painted ride,
With horses that jump from afar.

Each laugh's a flutter, soft and sweet,
Like cotton candy on the tongue,
We chase the light with playful feet,
While rhymes of yesteryears are sung.

The gears of time creak with delight,
As faces change like fleeting stars,
In this carousel of bright escape,
We swing and sway, no need for cars.

The Soft Song of Detached Memory

In the garden, laughter flies,
Colors tangled, tied, and wise.
Each small thing that drifts away,
Hums a tune of yesterday.

A sock parade under the sun,
With the clowns that dance and run.
Frolicking on the breeze's whim,
As dreams take shape and slowly swim.

Jingling joy, unkempt delight,
A mismatched world feels just right.
Floating cheer on every thread,
Whimsical paths that dance instead.

A moment lost but oh so sweet,
Bouncing paths, unexpected feet.
Memory's laugh, a playful tease,
In the sun, with care, we seize.

Frayed Edges and Gentle Currents

Worn-out patches start to sway,
In the breeze, they laugh and play.
Funky seams and wild designs,
Life's a canvas with no lines.

A curtain flutters, winks to me,
How silly things can light and flee.
Tangled tales in colors bright,
Frayed edges glow in morning light.

Little whispers flying high,
Painted dreams in the sky.
Each small tear holds a cheeky grin,
In this tapestry, we spin.

Mirthful moments, joyous fright,
Dance unbridled, take your flight.
In the chaos, find the fun,
Friended fabric for everyone.

Ephemeral Emblems in Flight

Giggles weave through the warm air,
Fleeting symbols, wild and rare.
Tossed and turned, they break like jokes,
Chasing whims of vibrant folks.

A paper hat on a wandering bee,
Joyful antics, wild and free.
Each sigh whispers tales to share,
Moments flutter, unaware.

Eager skirts dance with delight,
Swirling patterns of pure light.
Laughter lingers, hugs the ground,
In laughter's wake, joy is found.

Puppets on a breezy stage,
Life unfolds like an open page.
Bubbly dreams with silly schemes,
Dancing forth in tangled beams.

Lullabies of Tethered Fabric

Nestled snug in a quilt’s embrace,
Dreams tumble down without a trace.
Giggling stitches weave a tune,
As slumber drifts beneath the moon.

While curtains sway, the night awakes,
Whispers wander, gentle flake.
From patch to patch, the stories clump,
In sleepy threads, the heart will thump.

Amid soft chaos, joy’s sweet birth,
Silent giggles fill the earth.
A fabric's tale, a cozy plight,
Each lullaby embraces night.

Rest assured, the play's not done,
Tomorrow springs, with laughter spun.
Every fold hides a silly sound,
In our dreams, the giggles abound.

A Tangle of Airy Wonderments

A ladybug hat danced with glee,
Twisting around a gnarled tree.
The grasshoppers chuckled aloud,
As giggles floated from the crowd.

A ticklish breeze whispered a tune,
Carrying laughter beneath the moon.
A kite caught up in a game so grand,
Tangled now, it waved like a hand.

Marbles rolled off in a coherent spree,
Chasing each other, happy as can be.
A whistle blared from a nearby stall,
Making the others giggle and sprawl.

As dusk painted scenes in absurd delight,
Dreams fluttered free, taking flight.
A parade of oddities swayed in the air,
Spinning and twirling without a care.

Interlacing Echoes in the Wind

A rubber boot leapt, heel over toe,
Chasing along where the breezes blow.
Socks tangled up in a bouncy dance,
Unraveling tales while seeking a chance.

The yo-yo twirled in a dizzy spin,
As giggles echoed where fun begins.
Balloons floated, puffing with pride,
Waving their ribbons, a colorful ride.

An umbrella spun, caught in a jest,
Twirled by the wind, it thought it the best.
With giggly whispers and playful winks,
Silly happenings caught us in syncs.

In this raucous ballet of joy and cheer,
All the landscapes seemed to draw near.
What a merry jingle of sounds afloat,
In a world that squeaked and giddily wrote.

An Odyssey of Colors in Flight

A paper plane soared off with cheer,
Decorated with doodles, oh so dear.
Glittery trails left in the sky,
As it wanted to learn how to fly.

A rainbow winked, slipped on a cap,
While giggles placed it in a funny gap.
Colors dashed in gleeful parade,
Their legacy woven, never to fade.

A sunflower winked and swayed with glee,
Sprinkling whispers from a bumblebee.
With each petal dancing out its tale,
Creating a symphony, vivid and frail.

In this carnival of hues and zest,
Nature conspired, putting us to the test.
With laughter afloat on a vibrant spree,
The world grew whimsically, wild and free.

The Unseen Connection in Airborne Tales

A dandelion puff, so light and spry,
Whispered secrets as it drifted by.
Chasing the giggles of children at play,
In a cacophony of joy, they sway.

Marbles rolling down with a clatter,
Mismatched socks in a playful patter.
The wind hummed tunes and set hearts ablaze,
As silliness twirled in wind-blown frays.

A top hat spun on its balanced feet,
Juggling confetti—what a funny feat!
With rabbits in pockets, the audience roared,
As laughter and applause freely poured.

In quiet corners of laughter's domain,
There lived silly tunes that never waned.
With every gust, an adventure unfurled,
A tapestry woven in a dreamy world.

Threads of the Gentle Zephyr

A tiny pop, a gentle swirl,
The fabric flies, a playful twirl.
Laughing threads in a wild embrace,
Whispering secrets in a skyward chase.

Windy whispers, a playful tease,
Twirling camisoles, teasing peas.
Each soars up high, then dips with glee,
Wiggly knots dance joyfully free.

A tug here, a tickle there,
The lightest touch, a dash of flair.
Like tiny sprites having their say,
Laughing out loud, come join the play.

Around the trees, a merry thread,
Tangles and giggles till evening's red.
Soft as dreams on a breezy flight,
Each little laugh a spark of light.

Stitching Dreams with the Wind

Threads of Fun, they play and twist,
Out on the air, a light-hearted mist.
Soft as whispers, bold as a jest,
With every flutter, they come to rest.

Dancing fabrics chasing the sun,
With sprightly motions, they come undone.
Loop-de-loops in a swirling race,
Silly patterns all over the place.

The wind's a seamstress, deft and sly,
Snipping and stitching, oh me, oh my!
Giggling stitches, what a sight to see,
As laughter sways through each cotton tree.

Around and around, in joyful rides,
Fabrics flutter like playful tides.
In the heart of laughter's sweet caress,
Dreams are stitched with a bright finesse.

Laughter of Colorful Fasteners

Clips and clasps, a jolly band,
Flapping together, a merry stand.
Bottles pop, and giggles rise,
As they play tag beneath the skies.

Colors splash in a playful spree,
Twinkling, winking, in glee so free.
Each little snap, a ticklish way,
To dance with breezes in a bright ballet.

Fastening dreams, they skip and whirl,
Crafting laughter as they unfurl.
In a whirl of joy, they slide and spin,
The tiniest joys that make us grin.

From the pockets to the skies,
These tiny twinklers wear no disguise.
As laughter threads through every scene,
Fasteners vibrate in colors unseen.

The Dance of Tiny Adornments

Little jewels caught in the air,
Jangling laughter, a charming flair.
Whirling and twirling, oh what a sight,
Spinning around in dazzling light.

Pockets of mirth fly high and low,
A cheerful dance, a sparkling show.
With every flick, they all unite,
In a boisterous jig—what pure delight!

A clip here, a strap there, they groove,
Jesting about in a playful move.
Adorned in smiles, they giggle and play,
In the lighthearted breeze, they sway away.

From vest to cap, they take their chance,
Breezy fashion fuels every dance.
Among the giggles, in cheerful bliss,
These tiny treasures cannot resist.

Chasing Echoes of Soft Whims

A pocket full of giggles, I run,
Chasing laughter like a rolling stone.
Twirling hats that leap and dance,
As if they hold a secret chance.

Fluffy clouds tickle passing sights,
Swirling dandelions in silly flights.
I trip on dreams, a playful cheer,
Each bend whispers, 'Fun is near!'

Nonsensical boots tap to a beat,
As fluffy bunnies hop on light feet.
In a world where whimsy pays the toll,
I find the giggles that make me whole.

A carousel of random chatter,
Amidst the chaos, joy will scatter.
With a wink and nudge, I join the blast,
In the dance of echoes, free at last.

Secrets Carried by the Wind

A secret breeze whispers my name,
It juggles tales that play a game.
Sudden twirls of leaves take flight,
Winking slyly, oh what a sight!

Invisible whispers flee the trees,
Tickling noses, like ticklish bees.
Socks that dance without a pair,
Laughter's echo fills the air.

Muffin caps spinning down the lane,
Chasing memories, light as rain.
Windy whispers catch my coat,
I leap and laugh, a comical note.

Nonsense creatures skip and spin,
Carrying dreams where tales begin.
A tapestry of giggles around,
In this whirlwind, my joy is found.

Fabric Flutters in the Twilight

Breezy curtains wave and tease,
As stars play hide and seek with ease.
A patchwork quilt of frolicsome fun,
Each thread a giggle under the sun.

Silk pajamas dance with glee,
As night wraps its arms around the tree.
Twinkling stars join in the rhyme,
A bizarre jig, oh what a time!

Hats take off, and so do shoes,
Frolicking patterns, wild hues.
In twilight's charm, we jump and glide,
Letting whims and laughter collide.

With every twirl, secrets unfold,
In fabric dreams, adventures bold.
The night giggles, oh what a tease,
As joy flutters softly on the breeze.

Dreamy Gestures of Miniature Ties

Tiny ties with a wiggly flair,
Twisting and turning without a care.
A merry parade of buttons small,
With whimsical dances that enthrall.

Twirling figures in a playful toss,
Each tiny gesture, never a loss.
Miniature laughter is heard all around,
In a symphony soft, joy is found.

As shoelaces tie themselves in knots,
Chasing shadows, ignoring all plots.
Silly hats bob and weave with grace,
In this romp, I find my place.

Dreams wrapped tight in threads of delight,
Every turn brings shiny insight.
With grins so wide, we flirt with cheer,
In the land of giggles, adventure near.

The Symphony of Passing Trinkets

Tiny treasures flip and swirl,
Bright and bold, like a merry whirl.
A wink of flair in the morning glow,
They dance around, putting on a show.

From pockets stuffed with forgotten glee,
They leap and tumble, all wild and free.
A jingle here, a sparkle there,
A parade of laughter fills the air.

Will they fall? Will they fly?
Chasing dreams in the open sky.
With every twist, a tale to tell,
Of how they escaped from a dusty shell.

Their stories whisper on the breeze,
As they tease the branches of swaying trees.
In a whimsical world where fun is king,
These flying trinkets make our hearts sing.

A Canvas of Fluttering Souls

A patchwork quilt of colors bright,
Each little piece a pure delight.
They shimmy and shake, a playful riot,
Gathering laughter, oh, they can't be quiet.

Like confetti tossed on a sunny day,
They flit about, come what may.
A burst of glee in the hottest sun,
Who knew such joy could come from fun?

With a giggle here and a chuckle there,
They spin and twirl without a care.
In the gentle pull of a cheeky breeze,
Dodging raindrops just to tease.

They mingle with whims, so fresh and spry,
Creating art that reaches the sky.
In this gallery of giddy souls,
Each lively trinket plays their roles.

Nature's Fashioned Call

The earth discloses its playful charms,
With shiny bits that beckon and swarm.
Dressed in laughter, the wind takes hold,
Of quirky ornaments, both brave and bold.

Like feathers floating from a silly hat,
They swirl and dance, oh, imagine that!
In a breeze that plays with every spin,
Tickling the toes of the thickest skin.

As if the trees are giggling loud,
With every loop, they join the crowd.
A carnival in nature's embrace,
Where each shiny thing finds its place.

The symphony of nature's call,
With trinkets bouncing, we welcome all.
A spectacle of fun, that can't be missed,
In this playful dance, we all exist.

Delicate Trinkets in Flight

A flurry of sparkles takes to the sky,
With gleeful shivers, oh me, oh my!
Laughing as they whiz and glide,
Little wonders take us for a ride.

With every spin, a gleeful cheer,
Whirling memories, so bright, so clear.
They whisper secrets from memory's past,
In the jolly breeze, our hearts are cast.

Combatting the mundane with colorful flair,
Catching a ride in the fragrant air.
A playful army of little delights,
Transforming dull days into joyful sights.

So let's gather the pieces of fun we find,
Join the revelry of the whimsical kind.
In the fluttering party that nature leads,
We celebrate all with joyous deeds.

Renegade Symbols of Childhood

Tiny discs of laughter fly,
Pockets bursting, oh my, oh my!
Chasing dreams on a summer day,
With winks and giggles, come what may.

Crafted visions in a swirl,
Dizzy dancing, watch them twirl.
Each one whispers tales so loud,
As we parade, a giggling crowd.

A rally of mischief in flight,
Unexpected turns ignite delight.
Colors catch the golden sun,
In joyful chaos, we all run.

Fleeting moments drift like smoke,
As carefree spirits gently stoke.
Childhood whispers on the wing,
Oh, the joy that laughter brings!

A Mosaic of Reflections in the Air

Glimmering shapes in a daydream haze,
Reflecting the mischief of childhood's plays.
Twirling secrets, each one braves,
Lost in the dance of whimsical waves.

A jigsaw puzzle made of mirth,
Spinning memories of purest worth.
Children's laughter, the artist's brush,
Painting the world in a vibrant hush.

Wobbly creations drift and sway,
Tickling our hearts in a cheeky way.
Blowing kisses to the soft clouds,
While echoing giggles draw in the crowds.

Fragments of joy on a lingering sigh,
Like swirling confetti, they float and fly.
A patchwork of fun in the gentle air,
Dancing with wonder, without a care.

Stardust Strung on Tangents

Wink and twinkle, the evening starts,
Sprinkled laughter with mischievous hearts.
Glowing orbs spun from sunny dreams,
Hovering joy that giggles and beams.

Chasing shadows of playful schemes,
Arcane secrets wrapped in gleams.
Laughter echoes where dreams collide,
As starlit whispers tenderly glide.

Fleeting trails of sparkly heat,
Sassy vibes that can’t be beat.
Crafty patterns drawn in the sky,
Tickling whims as we flutter by.

Wandering spirits with gleeful tunes,
Swaying softly like bright balloons.
In this world, mirth finds its wings,
As we dance around with all the things.

The Wind's Play with Forgotten Charms

Gentle breezes tease and play,
With playful winks, they whirl away.
Forgotten trinkets, lost to time,
Stirring laughter, a joyful rhyme.

Echoes linger with a fabled tune,
Twisting secrets beneath the moon.
A riddle wrapped in sunshine's beam,
Crafty jokes woven in a dream.

Flitting whispers weave through the trees,
Swaying gracefully, like a tease.
Hover and flutter, invite the cheer,
Each turn a chuckle, every shift dear.

Dance with shadows, tap your feet,
Whimsical whispers, oh how sweet!
Embrace the moment, let spirits roam,
In this playful world, we find our home.

Lost Tokens in the Whispering Wind

A penny rolls, a quarter flies,
Through gusts of giggles, under the skies.
Laughter carries, as coins collide,
Chasing shadows, where secrets reside.

A button leaps from a pocket, bold,
Dancing away like a story untold.
With each little bounce, it starts to sing,
A tune of mischief, a joyous fling.

The wind, a jester with tricks to show,
Swirls up laughter like fluffy snow.
As treasures tumble, the chase begins,
In a world where whimsy always wins.

So gather your tokens, let spirits lift,
Join the wind's laughter, the greatest gift.
For in each fold, a joy unfurls,
In whispers of laughter, our heart twirls.

Fabrics of Echoing Laughter

In the fabric of twilight, threads intertwine,
Stitches of giggles that brightly shine.
With every gust, a new folly wakes,
Echoing joy, as the laughter breaks.

A quilt of chuckles, so whimsically sewn,
As twirls of delight in the breezes are blown.
Tickles of fabric, a tapestry spun,
With shades of jest under the sun.

From playful whispers and tales so grand,
The seams come alive, like a music band.
Woven in joy, with every thread,
A colorful story rises, pure joy spread.

So dance with the fibers, let spirits glide,
In the currents of laughter, we all must ride.
For in each seam, mirth we will find,
A canvas of joy, sweetly entwined.

Whispers of Wind and Fabric

A gentle breeze turns giggles to song,
As fabric flutters, where we belong.
With whispers of stories stitched in delight,
In the garden of laughter, everything's bright.

A handkerchief sails, like a kite on the run,
Spreading sweet laughter, oh what fun!
Tales twirl around with every swoosh,
As frolicsome breezes give giggles a push.

In this playful quilt, the wind takes its part,
Each ripple and rustle a note from the heart.
Mirthful moments, painted on air,
Echo through laughter, without a care.

So listen closely, to whispers unfold,
With each twist and turn, new tales are told.
For in the soft fabric of whimsy's caress,
Laughter’s the thread that binds us in zest.

Tales Woven in the Air

Breezes wrap stories, light as a feather,
Swirling together, each thread a tether.
Tales of silliness dance and delight,
Guiding our joys as they take flight.

A lost sock twirls, with a wink and a grin,
In the spin of the wind, where do we begin?
Whispers of mischief fill up the skies,
With laughter aloft, happiness flies.

Clotheslines shimmer with secrets untold,
Woven in warmth, colorful and bold.
Every flap and flutter brings giggles anew,
Tales like balloons in a sky bright and blue.

So come join the frolic, let spirits be free,
In the tales held aloft, just you wait and see.
For every soft whisper that floats through the air,
Is a promise of laughter, a moment to share.

Whimsical Winds and Their Tales

A gust goes by with a playful sigh,
It lifts my hat and makes it fly.
It tickles my ears, just like a tease,
As I chase my thoughts on a wobbly breeze.

Invisible hands have taken their rest,
With laughter so loud, they put me to test.
A jiggle, a wiggle, oh what a sight,
The wind's a comedian, pure delight!

In the park, it swirls with delight,
Dancing the leaves, oh what a sight!
Mischief afoot, it won't say bye,
While I stumble and trip as I try to comply.

With every gust, a tale is spun,
A game of tag with no set run.
The world spins ‘round with each wild push,
Leaving us laughing in a joyful hush.

Echoes of a Tailored Journey

On paths well trodden, the wind does sway,
With tales unspooled in a curious way.
A sock drifts by, then a mitten too,
It seems my laundry’s gone walkin’ anew!

The scarves commence a silly dance,
While jackets twirl as if in a trance.
Each flurry a giggle, a wiggle, a shout,
As I chase them down, filled with laughter and doubt.

I swear I spotted a shoe in the air,
A rogue, taking flight without a care.
Though I'm left with only mismatched pairs,
I'll keep on smiling; life's full of snares!

As echoes linger, we laugh and cheer,
For every lost item, a new memory near.
So here’s to the journey and all its flair,
As we follow the whispers that swirl everywhere.

Celestial Threads Unfurled

Gossamer strands dance in the light,
Spinning through clouds, oh what a sight!
A sock from the laundry sweeps past the moon,
Its pair left behind, singing a tune.

Across the sky, a button takes flight,
With dreams entwined in the soft evening light.
They gallivant forth, a mess of odd flair,
Reminding us all that we're free as the air.

Each twinkle above has a giggle beneath,
As tales of the shimmery fabrics bequeath.
The world's a loom, weaving paths dense and rare,
With laughter and yarn, we're all part of the fair.

So let's twirl through stardust and chase that thrill,
Collecting each moment, what joy we fulfill!
For in this grand tapestry, we're all playful threads,
Connected by laughter, where nonsense spreads.

Soft Murmurs of Attached Memories

In a gentle breeze, whispers arise,
With tales of the past, oh where memory flies.
The hat that I wore with its fluffy old brim,
Sways with the giggles, so modest and prim.

A rogue shoelace dances, full of surprise,
Reminding of childhood, where laughter will rise.
The breeze takes a snip from my old favorite shirt,
Spinning with joy like a happy dessert.

Echoes of chatter cling like sweet honey,
As a few stray balloons rise up, oh so funny!
Floating together, those memories bright,
In the chaos of joy, there's an unending light.

So let's gather the moments, old stories and more,
In this whimsical world, we can always explore.
For every soft murmur speaks straight to the heart,
We're stitched together by laughter, that's art!

Carried Away by a Gentle Draft

A hat danced high on the wind's soft laugh,
Chased by a sock, what a curious gaff!
They twirled and spun in a whimsical race,
With a jig and a jiggle, they put on a face.

The sun winked down at the playful display,
As a scarf joined in, brightening the fray.
What joy there is in a gust's light embrace,
Turning laundry into a merry, wild chase!

A slip of a breeze, and the loose change flies,
Dimes roll along, oh, how they surprise!
They tumble and tumble, oh where do they go?
Sliding and gliding in a whirling show.

So take off your hat, let it jump if it pleases,
For when winds are fickle, laughter just increases.
Embrace the delight as the air comes alive,
With twirls and soft giggles, we joyously strive.

The Echoing Chorus of Little Things

A button popped off, and it giggled with glee,
Rolling away, oh, where could it be?
It danced on the countertop, plinked on the floor,
Chasing after crumbs, oh, it wanted more!

The keys chimed in, all jingly and bright,
Joining the button in its comical flight.
A spoon did a flip, and the fork joined the fun,
Together they twirled, under the midday sun.

The fridge hummed along, a symphony grand,
As the kitchen utensils all started a band.
A spatula waved, with a grin on its face,
While the clock kept the time, at a hilarious pace.

Each little item, with a personality bold,
Brought laughter and joy as their stories unfold.
In the chorus of mischief, they danced all around,
Echoes of chuckles were the sweetest of sounds.

A Breeze Through the Stitchery

In a cozy old corner where fabrics reside,
The wind slipped inside with a playful stride.
It rustled the quilts and it ruffled the threads,
Spinning tales of adventures, like tea parties in beds.

A needle popped up with a wink and a nod,
While threads told their stories, a little bit odd.
They tangled in giggles, like kids at a fair,
Mismatched patterns blooming in the light summer air.

The seam ripper laughed as it joined in the fun,
Untangling chaos, oh, wasn't it a run!
Each patch had a voice that was filled with delight,
As they swirled through the room like a soft kite in flight.

So let the breeze wander through yonder and here,
Bringing fabric and laughter, oh, let’s give a cheer!
In the stitchery's heart, where all joys interlace,
A witty parade spins with magical grace.

Ties that Waft Beyond Boundaries

A bow tie took flight with style and flair,
Whirling and twirling, it danced in the air.
With a waltz of the collar, oh, what a sight!
Ties flapping wildly, bringing giggles to light.

A belt joined the brawl, with a shimmy and sway,
Taking on the roles in their silly ballet.
They leaped from the table, oh, what a charade!
As capes and neckties began a parade.

The suspenders chimed in with a raucous good cheer,
Calling for buttons to join and appear.
With a tug and a pull, they formed a grand crew,
Navigating air currents like pros, oh so true!

In a tale of these ties, joy floats in the wind,
As laughter and mischief become the best friends.
So loosen your grip, let the laughter take hold,
For a journey with style is a joy to behold!

Threads Meandering Through Time

In a world of cloth and thread,
The quirkiest tales are often spread.
A lost penny sings in the rain,
While socks conspire to cause us pain.

Grandma's quilt spins yarns of cheer,
With every stitch, a smile appears.
Oh, the mischief that they weave,
In fabric land, we dare believe.

Lace that tickles and charms the toes,
Secrets hidden in knotted bows.
A rogue seam serves a laugh or two,
With every bobble, delight shines through.

Spools of laughter roll off the shelf,
In threads of joy, we find ourselves.
The tapestry of life is bright,
As time dances in colors light.

Captured in a Gentle Drift

A paper boat winks at the sun,
With a giggle, it sails for fun.
Naps are taken under the tree,
As shadows flicker, wild and free.

Merry melodies ride the air,
Whispers of mischief everywhere.
Leaves play tag with breezy sighs,
As dandelions dance and rise.

A wayward cap catches my eye,
With tales of journeys to the sky.
Tickling laughter fills the breeze,
As nature creates whimsical tease.

Every drift brings giggles anew,
Floating dreams of a merry crew.
Laughter glides on a gentle wave,
In this drift, we joyfully rave.

The Ephemeral Trade of Tiny Ornaments

In the market of lost little charms,
Jests and trinkets lend their arms.
A shoe that's small, but oh so spry,
Winks at passersby with a sigh.

Marbles gossip, rolling away,
Whispering secrets of yesterday.
Tiny keys unlock the heart,
With every exchange, we play our part.

Fringe and flare in a curious pile,
Catching our laughter with every mile.
A mismatch of colors, a playful sight,
In this trade, everything feels right.

Silly hats tip to the crowd,
As whimsical spirits shout out loud.
Ornaments laughing, reflecting the day,
In a fun fair of delights on display.

Dreamlike Currents of Kinship

In a realm where giggles flow,
Connected by laughter, we grow.
Stars twinkle in our playful rhyme,
As we drift through the currents of time.

Mismatched socks find their pair,
In the warmth of the love we share.
Giggling dreams hang like laundry bright,
Crafting a tapestry of delight.

An old kite sways with glee on a line,
In the dreamscape where all things shine.
We toast to the moments that tease and twirl,
In this whimsical fabric, we unfurl.

With laughter that dances like stars in the night,
Every bond feels ever so light.
In currents of kinship, we glide and play,
Embracing the fun in our own quirky way.

Facets of Airborne Creativity

Giggling clouds toss thoughts on high,
As laughter flutters, watch ideas fly.
A twist of whimsy in every gust,
Dancing with dreams, we can’t help but trust.

A kite misplaced, a silly hat,
Cheeky winds blow, what about that?
With giggles soaring, we slice the air,
Imagination blooms; it’s everywhere!

Twirling notions, a wacky race,
Like ducks in bowties, they all embrace.
A carnival ride on a soft feather,
With a tickle of joy that brings us together.

Whirls of colors in a comical chase,
Echoes of laughter, a cheerful space.
Sprinkles of madness and loud surprise,
Catch the delight with our wide-open eyes.

Tethered to the Whisper of Change

A rumbling giggle as the winds begin,
Shuffling ideas, let the fun spin in.
A flutter of chaos in a gentle dance,
Wrapped in surprise; give life a chance.

Umbrellas bright like jellybeans soar,
Each gust a chuckle that begs for more.
Whispers of mischief on a summer's day,
Painting the world in a colorful way.

Dandelions laugh, seeds whirl around,
Tickling grass where giggles are found.
Held by the whim of a playful breeze,
Forever dancing, doing as they please.

Puppets of change, our laughter in tow,
Chasing the twilight where silliness flows.
So tethered to joy, we joyously sing,
With the whispers of change, we take flight in spring.

Nature’s Dance of Soft Embellishments

Fluffy whimsy floats up and away,
Draped in giggles, what a buffet!
Leaves in a line, the smallest parade,
A trickster's game that nature has played.

Butterflies chuckle; they flutter in pairs,
Bouncing on breezes without any cares.
A splash of color, a tangle of fun,
Nature’s delight, a race just begun.

With each twist and turn, mishaps abound,
As flowers get tangled, they spin round and round.
A hush and a buzz, the garden awakes,
In a jig of delight, it dances, and shakes.

Silly the shadows that play hide and seek,
While sprinkles of laughter burst forth to peek.
Embellished by nature in every embrace,
Our hearts beat to rhythm in this funny place.

The Gentle Spirit of Woven Dreams

Threads of laughter in the cool night air,
A tangle of wishes, no hearts to spare.
Twirled in the breeze, a tapestry bright,
Weaving soft stories under the starlight.

The moon beams down, with a smirk on its face,
As giggles echo in this wondrous space.
With every stitch, a chuckle is sewn,
In the quilt of the night, we feel right at home.

Spirits of play dance lightly and free,
Tickling the edges of dreams we see.
Woven together, each thought takes flight,
Wrapped in the joy of a whimsical night.

Laughter, it lingers, a gentle refrain,
Easing the world; we lose and gain.
With every stitch of our crafted dreams,
Funny and bright, or so it seems.

Sailing Through Threads of Time

On a sail of colorful thread,
I drift where the giggles spread.
With each tug of a rain-soaked string,
I laugh at the chaos the breezes bring.

Time dances while I hold my course,
With a knot of laughter, I feel its force.
Each gust a jester in the sunlit blue,
I'm just a fool, sailing through.

A patchwork quilt of tales I weave,
Like a pirate ship with a grand reprieve.
Throw me those wishful pens and ink,
I'll write my story before we blink.

So join me on this merry ride,
Where threads of folly become my guide.
We'll skip through moments, swirl and glide,
On the tales of joy, let's take pride.

Timeless Fables in the Air

In the sky, tales fly like kites,
Whispered stories of silly sights.
A floppy hat and clumsy shoes,
Humor blooms where laughter brews.

Fairy tale mishaps high above,
Sailing on sighs, a breeze of love.
A dragon sneezed, the knight lost his hat,
Chasing down stories where the giggles splat.

Clouds don wigs, they prance and spin,
While owls in glasses chuckle within.
Fables linger like echoes of glee,
In a timeless realm that's wild and free.

So let’s toss our worries, lean back and stare,
At the joyful fables whispering in the air.
With each twist and turn, we’ll make a new friend,
In this laughter-filled tale that will never end.

Serenade of the Flying Trinkets

A chorus sways—trinkets in flight,
Dancing in twirls—a marvelous sight.
A thimble spins on the breeze like a dream,
While a paper clip joins in the gleam.

The laughter rings as they scatter and dive,
In a wacky ballet that feels so alive.
A tiny bell jingles while spinning around,
In the realm of whimsy, joy is unbound.

Oh, the spoons and forks in a wild parade,
Giggling colorful dreams as they wade.
Caught in a loop of joyous delight,
These flying treasures sparkle grace in flight.

So let's join their extravaganza up high,
With unrestrained laughter, oh my, oh my!
As we serenade these trinkets so free,
In the playful winds, we find our glee.

Unraveled Stories Underneath the Sky

Beneath a sky of roguish hues,
Live tales unwound in laughter's muse.
A sock on a cat, slipping with flair,
Tickles the clouds with stories to share.

Each whimsy wrapped in a twisty line,
Frolicsome plots on the rise, divine.
A plucky hat hops and bounces about,
While giggles erupt from the dog down south.

Time flickers bright with a chuckling sound,
As each tale unravels, joy is found.
Oddball adventures, a guaranteed hit,
From mere moments, we craft a splendid skit.

So, join in the fun, let your spirit fly,
Underneath the raucous and radiant sky.
With unending stories weaving high and low,
Laughter’s our compass, let’s go with the flow.

Fleeting Adornments on the Gales

A weathervane twirls in glee,
Chasing round like a clumsy bee.
Trousers flap in a playful dance,
While mismatched socks spin in a chance.

The laughter of kites fills the air,
As hats take flight without a care.
A scarf wraps itself 'round the dog,
While kids giggle, lost in the fog.

Balloons bob on the lightest sigh,
With dreams as big as the endless sky.
A dandelion puff whispers away,
And the world spins in a joyful ballet.

So let the whimsies take their flight,
On breezes that spark pure delight.
Life’s quirks wear a smile, so bright,
In a carnival of fabric, quite a sight.

Patterns Stirred in the Warmth of Motion

A polka-dot scarf snags on a tree,
As quirky as a squirrel, oh so free.
The plaid shirt flutters, a raucous cheer,
Drawing laughter from all who come near.

A cape cascades with style so bold,
Its owner just tripped—now who's being told?
A whimsical dance in every corner,
As the sunlight glows, life's true performer.

Ties twist and tangle, a sight to behold,
Like gossiping friends sharing tales untold.
The playful chaos teems with delight,
In a world where everything feels just right.

The breeze is a jester, playful and sly,
Creating mischief as it glides by.
In this circus of motion, laughter rings,
With patterns and colors like dreams on wings.

Sails of the Serene

A shirt sails high on the breeze’s song,
Laughing as it drifts, where it belongs.
Kites soar above, with tails in a twirl,
As children chase giggles and give the world a whirl.

A hat takes off, leads a merry chase,
Dusting off troubles in light-hearted grace.
Swirling skirts join the breeze’s own tune,
As everyone twirls ‘neath the glow of the moon.

With skirts that swirl and shoes that glide,
This party of motion, we cannot hide.
In a tapestry rich with laughter and cheer,
The gales spread joy like confetti each year.

So dance with the whims that the zephyr sends,
In this joyous world, where laughter transcends.
Life’s gentle sails embrace with ease,
In a sea of soft fabric on playful degrees.

A Symphony of Wayward Closures

Zippers hum a tune, a quirky refrain,
As shoelaces trip up, it's all in good gain.
The buttons chatter with boisterous cheer,
While socks play hide and seek, oh dear!

An umbrella's floppy dance in the rain,
Brings giggles and grins, we can't help but feign.
Coats that flap like wings of a bird,
In this silly symphony, odd notes are heard.

Belt buckles jingle, a merry little sound,
As laughter echoes throughout the playground.
With pockets stuffed with whimsical dreams,
Life’s a parade bursting at the seams.

Close your eyes, and feel the rejoice,
In a world where fabric sings with a voice.
So let’s embrace every twist and turn,
As laughter ignites and our hearts brightly burn.

Colors in Motion with the Gale

Chasing rainbows through the trees,
A wild dance with every breeze.
Clotheslines jiggle, oh what fun,
As socks and shirts go on the run.

Twisting, turning, up in flight,
A pair of mittens take their height.
Giggles echo, laughter sings,
As hats play tag with all the flings.

Scarves are swirling like a kite,
A polka dot parade in sight.
The wind's a jester, bold and bright,
With colors flashing day and night.

Who knew fashion could take wings?
In this chaos, pure joy springs.
A sight so silly, hearts do swell,
As nature spins its funny spell.

A Melody of Suspended Whispers

Whispers travel through the air,
With secrets dancing everywhere.
A sock serenade, oh such a tune,
As laundry flutters under the moon.

Silk and cotton gently sway,
Chirpy notes of cloth ballet.
A chorus rises, soft and sweet,
As mismatched socks choose to compete.

Tangled in a waltz of fun,
What stories could these fabrics spun?
Winds compose a silly song,
As flapping rags join in along.

With every twist the laughter grows,
In this concert, anything goes.
A melody of joy, quite clear,
As whispers dance from ear to ear.

Fluttering Wishes on the Wind

Wishes flutter on a whim,
As breezes play, both bold and dim.
A paper kite takes off with glee,
While napkins float like poetry.

Silly dreams of toasting bread,
Run wild in winds, away they spread.
A race of hats, a comical sight,
As they zoom past with sheer delight.

Balloons burst forth in vibrant cheer,
With giggles echoing far and near.
Whimsical flights of fancy soar,
While snacks are swept up from the floor.

With every gust, a chuckle blends,
As laughter on the breeze transcends.
Oh, fluttering wishes, take your flight,
In the windy realm of pure delight.

The Lightness of Tethered Dreams

Dreams are tied with threads of air,
As giggles float without a care.
A jumping bean in a wobbly chase,
With bouncing hopes all over the place.

Tethered wishes soaring high,
A comedy of driftwood by.
Hats in tow, oh what a sight,
As dreams balloon with pure delight.

A tumble here, a twirl over there,
As laughter fills the sunny air.
Socks and gloves take off their shoes,
In this realm, there's nothing to lose.

Each little giggle tugs a string,
As lightness makes our hearts take wing.
With tethered dreams, we prance and plod,
Reveling in the joy of odd.

Whispers of Stitches in the Wind

A button rolled down a grassy hill,
Chasing a laugh, with a quirky thrill.
It tripped on a twig, did a silly spin,
What a jolly sight, where to begin?

A thread of laughter floated by,
Whirling and twirling, oh my oh my!
It tangled with daisies, danced with delight,
A party of stitches, such a funny sight!

Two shank buttons wobbled, doing the jig,
One lost its shine, went down a fig.
With a wink and a smile, it waved goodbye,
"I've got a date with a bird in the sky!"

Laughter erupted, as a snap popped free,
From a pocket of dreams, wild and carefree.
They spun with the clouds, in joyous mayhem,
A festival of threads, where fun finds its gem.

Tapestry of Floating Dreams

Once there were buttons, in line for a ride,
Giggling together, feeling so spry.
They hitched a lift on a breezy cart,
Where every giggle played a part.

A twinkling button burst into song,
"Let's zip through the air, it won't be long!"
A ribbon joined in, dancing so bold,
They swirled into laughter, a sight to behold!

A pinched collar snickered, "Hey, watch my flair!"
As it flipped and flopped without a care.
With each little plink, a snicker arose,
Such playful antics, everybody knows!

In this tapestry of giggles and threads,
Where silliness reigns, and laughter spreads.
They twine and they twirl, like clouds in a swarm,
Creating a whimsy that keeps us warm.

Fickle Threads of Summer Air

A patch of sunshine brought out a smile,
Sills and seams danced, in the breeze for a while.
With a flip-flop here and a wiggle there,
Socks and buttons flew without a care.

The chorus of giggles floated around,
As hatpins joined in with a leap and a bound.
Each twinkling accent took to the air,
Creating a ruckus, a whimsical flare!

A button turned red, claiming it's shy,
While others were bold, reigning high in the sky.
They raced each other, such a comical chase,
Threads pulling tight in this wide-open space.

As the sun dipped low, they gathered in cheer,
With whispers of giggles, they all drew near.
In fickle threads, silliness spun,
A tapestry woven, where joy is the fun.

A Dance of Lost Fasteners

A lone fastener flopped, then took a grand leap,
"Let's throw a party, it's air I must keep!"
With a clink and a clatter, they gathered around,
Where laughter burst forth, a jubilant sound.

The snaps joined the dance, showing off flair,
A jig that was silly, without any care.
With whimsical rhythms, they scuttled about,
Spinning in joy, there was never a doubt!

From pants to the shirt, they twirled and they spun,
A raindrop of mirth, like heat from the sun.
Each little fastener found friendship in flight,
Creating a ruckus, what pure delight!

While shadows were dancing with glee in the night,
Fasteners whispered, "This feels just right!"
They rolled and they juked till the stars twinkled bright,
In this dance of lost fasteners, pure joy took flight.

Dancing Sprigs in the Sun

In fields of green where sunlight beams,
Little sprigs dance in silly dreams.
They twirl and wiggle, laugh and sway,
Chasing shadows of a perfect day.

With every gust, they take a chance,
Bouncing briskly, starting a prance.
A spin, a hop, they're light as air,
In this wild waltz, they shed all care.

The flowers giggle, the grass will hum,
As daisies join, creating a drum.
Each fluttering leaf, a partner to find,
In this merry chorus, all are entwined.

As evening falls, they giggle still,
Chasing dusk with an endless thrill.
In the twilight, they wink and slide,
These dancing sprigs, forever wide.

The Journey of a Floating Emblem

A little badge, so bright and round,
Glides through the air without a sound.
It wobbles here, it twirls back there,
On a wild ride, without a care.

It spies a cloud, says, "Come on, mate!"
While soaring high, it dreams of fate.
A gust of wind gives it a spin,
On this strange journey, let's begin!

Past birds and kites, it takes a flight,
Chasing sunshine, just out of sight.
With every swirl, it starts to grin,
Dancing through realms where dreams begin.

At last, it lands on a child's hat,
Then off they go, a chitchat spat.
The emblem smiles as stories weave,
In this shared laughter, they both believe.

Ephemeral Memories in the Wind

Caught up in whispers of playful air,
Fleeting echoes of moments rare.
They giggle softly, these tales take flight,
Fleeting memories, lost from sight.

As breezes beckon, they twirl and dance,
Sharing secrets in a cheeky glance.
The past frolics on wild currents bold,
Wrapped in laughter, stories told.

With every gust, a chuckle spills,
Tickling the heart, igniting thrills.
Like cotton candy, so sweet and bright,
These breezy tales all take to flight.

Yet soon they'll vanish, laugh and tease,
Slipping away with perfect ease.
But in the heart, they leave a glow,
Ephemeral whispers, a bright tableau.

Sojourn of Levity and Fabric

In a fabric land where smiles sprout,
A sojourn starts, filled with a route.
Threads of joy weaving along,
Tickling your heart with a vibrant song.

Cotton clouds and linen dreams,
Frolicking freely in sunlit beams.
With every stitch, the laughter grows,
Creating patterns, as friendship flows.

Amongst the seams, a jester glows,
Spinning tales wherever it goes.
It woos the wind to join in jest,
In this spirited world, they are blessed.

As daylight fades, the colors gleam,
A patchwork glimmer, a wild dream.
Sojourn of laughter, joy entwined,
In a fabric world, love's defined.

www.ingramcontent.com/pod product compliance
Lightning Source LLC
Chambersburg PA
CBHW070006300426
43661CB00141B/266
9781805861744